OBAMASUTRA

OBAMASUTRA

ILLUSTRATED

Volume 1

Insults for Special Occasions

ILYA KATZ

iUniverse, Inc.
Bloomington

OBAMASUTRA
VOLUME 1: INSULTS FOR SPECIAL OCCASIONS

iUniverse books may be ordered through booksellers or by contacting:

iUniverse
1663 Liberty Drive
Bloomington, IN 47403
www.iuniverse.com
1-800-Authors (1-800-288-4677)

ISBN: 978-1-4620-6823-4 (sc)
ISBN: 978-1-4620-6825-8 (hc)
ISBN: 978-1-4620-6824-1 (ebk)

Printed in the United States of America

iUniverse rev. date: 11/21/2011

For more information, please visit:
www.obamasutrabook.com

> *Here are I am.*
> *I stand at the door and knock.*
> *If you hear my voice*
> *and open the door,*
> *I will come.*
>
> *Revelations 3:20*

DEDICATION

Irving Berlin's song:
"God Bless America"
A sentiment I shout out.

Ilya Katz,
Satirist General.

25 years ago, I was seriously involved in Ronald Reagan's campaign, and today my book of conservative political insults "Obamasutra"—a satirical "KATZSCAN" of leftist politics is my act of responsibility and contribution to our struggle for freedom and prosperity of our country. With respect to the great man, eternally alive Ronald Reagan.

Dr. Ilya Katz,
With deepest appreciation for your generosity,

Ronald Reagan

Congratulations to freedom fighters—
CCC
Courageous Concerned Citizens
of "tea parties".
Today when "tea parties" reflect all the
layers of our society, it is time to transform
them into the "Coffee with milk" movement.
Every responsible rightist must catch two
lost in the dark leftists, enlighten them,
and convert them to the right faith.
Let us call it "1+2".

My name is Ilya Katz.

I am a political refugee from the Soviet Union, a former professor, director, journalist
and speaker.

I ran thousands of miles to get away from
a socialist "paradise", and do not want after 34 years to find myself back in it.

I was one of the millions of slaves forced to build the Socialist Tower of Babel.

Personally, I prefer the Capitalist
Tower of Pisa: it leans, but doesn't fall.

For many years, I was a prisoner
of conscience. Today, I do not want to be
a prisoner of nonsense.

A life without a future left terrible fingerprints on my throat.

I am not afraid of suffering from "Obamism,"
because I was already circumcised, financially
and politically oppressed in the land of socialism.

For 30 years, I have been a proud senior citizen
of the United States of America, retired but not
retarded.

As a father of four and grandfather of three,
if not me, *who* will take a stand for their future?

This book was created by inspiration from
the "achievements" of our President and his
accomplices.

If you throw such sharp aphorisms
at the White House windows, the glass will crack.

Acknowledgments

My greatest appreciation goes to FOX News,
described as *fair* and *balanced, Xerox,*
without tongue polishing, that produces
exact, truthful copies
of our reality.

I'm a small, ordinary potato, enlightened by FOX
News and will do the best
to see that satirical sparks presented in this book
will ignite an unstoppable fire of *reconquista* against
the coming Dark Ages.

Many thanks to Bill O'Reilly, Glenn Beck, Sean
Hannity, Greta von Sustern, Michael Huckabee,
Laura Ingraham, Geraldo Rivera, and others. We are
saying to socialism:
"No pasarán."

I don't care about a little dirty war
from the White (red) House.

If they try to hit the truthful, objective media below
the belt,
it does not matter how tall the pedestal is.
They are midgets.
It is too bad, but the swine flu of indifference is not
only around us; it's inside us.
But straight truth is our self-defense.
I hope that my song of protest won't turn out to be
a swan song.

DEAR READER,

A good quote
can express your thoughts most aptly;
so be our guest to toss these barbs
in your fight against injustice.
Stay tall, and God bless your position.
Here are some laughs, through tears,
wise vs. otherwise, guts vs. nuts.

This'll alarm you!
A small nuclear suitcase
containing common sense was lost.
I've found it.

It is tough to live without conscience,
but it is harder to live with one.

I can live with what I disagree with.
I can't live with what I'm forced to agree with.

The highest form of courage
is honest creativity.

I am an optimist and therefore believe
a drinking glass
of our political and economic life
is half-full, not half-empty.

Kindness is supposed
to possess quite strong fists.

As a philosopher once said:
"You must choose either to love people
or just to know them.
There is nothing in between."
I cannot accept that.
I love people. I study them.
And I offer my recipe
to improve homo sapiens and make them grow
from *homo vulgaris* to *homo patriotis*.

Caution—Explosive!
Sharp mind ahead.

Humor is when people laugh
at the one who fell;
satire is when people bully
the one who pushed.

All jokes that hit above the belt are humor;
those, hitting below it are satire.

An aphorism is a thorny flower
with deep roots.

A political aphorism reminds one
of an iceberg:
The smaller part is visible on the surface,
but the bigger part lies hidden underwater.

Nature does not tolerate a vacuum.
That is why
the position vacated by the incompetent one,
is immediately occupied by another.

Satire is truth in life-threatening doses.

Satire is a chemical that dissolves
the trust in idols.

I have a strong desire
to express myself,
despite knowing
it might be best to shut up.
Before, I just loved
freedom of thought.
Now, I wish to experience
the freedom of published thought. So,
save time and read my aphorisms.
They contain
the whole history of today's life.

Fellow Americans,
Tell me who you have voted for
and I will tell you who you are.

If America is a truck
and Obama is a trucker,
a citizen is a mother . . . sucker

If you want to be smart
and see things clearly,
take off your rose-colored glasses.

Chapter 1
Anti-American Idol

> *You shall not make for yourself
> an idol.*
>
> *Exodus 20:4*

There is a finger pointing at us.
Did anyone take the fingerprint?

Mr. Obama,
Katz
is on your back!!!

The true face of our God
was recognized
only when he acquired
the presidential image.

If we want to damage
our ruler's reputation, it is enough to tell the
truth about him.
Why lie?
The truth is far more damaging.

There is no explosion
more dangerous
than the explosion of fairness.

Obama is an idolator . . .
he worships himself.

Our God has one goal:
to remain on Olympus;
he does not care
about the people beneath.

Beware that new historical process does
not end up as criminal proceedings.

Triumph of the emperor without clothes,
surrounded by sellers of recycled, rotten
political merchandise.
He will, however,
enjoy a very short marathon.

Political retardation
starts from the mental one.

Our President is color blind:
he sees everything in red.

Our President is great . . .
like the seven deadly sins.

There is only one step
from laughter to sadness.
But from sadness to laughter . . .
four years.

"Obama is a thinker . . ."???

We are trying to understand
the anatomy of power
by studying the body
of the emperor without clothes.

He who has God on his lips,
sometimes has Devil in his heart.

Obama swore on the Bible
his pledge of allegiance . . . to the Koran.

Satire is more effective
than psychiatry in the treatment
of a progressive Napoleonic Complex.

Obama is our President.
That isn't a position—it's a diagnosis.

All dictators of all peoples and times
make this error:
They confuse the concept of "state"
with that of "homeland."
They also want us to make the same mistake.

Our Chief-of-Mischief pinches the balls
of the entire population,
and soon they will not only sing soprano
but will also howl like a wolf.

"We've got a dream . . . we've got a dream." Yes, but
somehow it turned into a nightmare.
Obama, however, does not have a dream
-he is already Obama.

Mr. Obama, didn't I once see you
in a movie theatre . . .
starring in a cartoon?

Could we touch our God?
Sure, but I hope
red dirt won't stick to our hands.

The inscription
on King Solomon's ring said:
"This, too, shall pass."
But this is not quite true.
It will pass only
if we won't get tired of fighting.
As the old saying goes:
"For the devil to win, it
is required only
that good people do nothing."

Today,
America without politicians, is
like a circus without clowns.

An American Tragedy is when the stage is occupied for four years by the production of a farce . . .

The mirror reflected the truth
of our leader's attempts
to appear to be a famous reformer.
He is, in fact, not a reformer . . .
he is only a performer.

Particularly Americans respect
those politicians
whose images appear on money.

World respects
George Washington
for all the good he did
as the father of our nation,
and Abraham Lincoln
for all the good he did
with his honesty and principles,
and Barack Obama
for his Nobel Prize.

NARCISSUS
LAUREATE

Mr. Obama,
the more often you see yourself
as an ideal,
the farther away you get from it.

Though Obama opened up new paths,
he forgot to put up road signs.

Our smart President has an answer
to every question and every problem.
Unfortunately, that is all he has.

In order to make the current mess
look beautiful, Obama is scaring our society
with the future.

A mountain gave birth to a mouse
and now the mouse is attempting
to give birth to a new epoch.

Irreplaceable people are those
who won't allow substitutes for themselves.

Let us love and cherish Mr. Obama.
If nothing else, he is our common mistake.

The same smiling face on T-shirts,
calendars, puzzles, figurines, drinks
and even hamburgers reflects
our beloved President.
It's full-blown Obamamania.
Why not create
a chocolate Obama filled with nuts?
At least his admirers can lick
any spot on his body.
Or how about a perfume:
"Scent of Obama?"

Mr. Obama offers transparency in words . . .
but a cover-up in actions.

Follow the crowd, it is the best way to get lost.

No matter
what kind of fences our President builds,
the people will still find the gaps.
Only after the removing of the fences
will the gaps disappear.

From the point of view of the Optimist-in-Chief,
the harder one falls down,
the greater the proof of his tallness of stature.

A pilot can be a good parachutist, but
a parachutist is always a bad pilot.

The President heads up
a powerful team . . .
of brainwashed impotents.

Mr. President,
if you really have a plan
to save America,
I suggest you leave it
in draft form
and don't show it to anybody;
it will really help our country.

Our President
is like a chess player who,
while losing the game,
states that he has
a winning position.

Our Democrats and
wishful impotents proclaim:
"Yes we can!"
Sorry, but you can't—
reply Republicans.

"To be or not to be?"

Not every monument
has a deep significance.
It is too easy to find the one,
that is just a lousy figure,
raised high on a pedestal.

It is half a disaster
when a loser holds a position
as a community organizer.
It is a full-blown disaster
when a loser comes
to the peak of power.

A Giant in position
can still be a Lilliputian by persuasion.

**Mr. Obama makes himself taller
by standing on the throat of the nation.**

Obama's ideas will retire
much earlier than their author.

Nobody can take away
Obama's talent to govern.
Why?
Because, to begin with,
he doesn't have it.

The President is a slave to ideas,
rather than a master of deeds.

Obama is not an innovator.
He is a lousy imitator.

A dangerous sickness is safer
than an unskilled doctor.

Since Obama can roll up mountains,
keep him away from them.

Mr. Obama craves public acknowledgement.
But that means that fools
acknowledge him too!

If Obama is a genius,
that is not a step forward by a culture,
one the future rests on,
but a step on which the present stumbles.

Obama cannot generate anything
except an impression.

In the world of politics, our President thinks
that he is a first-rate star.
The world thinks that he is at the fourth stage.

Obama's attempt to gain success
among Republicans
is similar to fishing in a community pool.

The headless horseman is especially dangerous
when leading the army.

Often, we take for a leader the runner,
who fell far behind in the previous race.

When an engineer looks for new ways
to drive the train,
it derails.

The president works as a compass
in a lost country.
He can walk through the rain and come out dry.

Obama is no Socrates, yet there are few things
about which he thinks he has no clue.

Our President tried to sell us
on the pristine quality of his views.
Unfortunately,
they are not very fresh,
and who will trust a dealer
with secondhand goods?

Selling secondhand merchandise
as new is possible
only through cheating.

Mr. Obama, even the best mistakes
do not need to be repeated.

Obama's reforms are dying
to become socialistic traditions.

Obama fights with old stereotypes
for the victory of new socialist ones.

The more Obama promises,
the more he takes away.

Obama attempts to redraw
the capitalistic world, as a bad editor does
with a manuscript, he cannot understand.

Obama suggested universal disarmament.
I want to believe that, at least,
he will not take away Cupid's arrows.

Obama's reforms remind me of diarrhea,
which never brings anything good along with it
and never happens at a good time.

You cannot feed the country with just promises,
though Obama himself eats just fine.

Idealists try to crawl into your soul,
and materialists into your pocket.
Obama knows how to crawl into our souls
first . . . and then into our pockets.

Obama quickly harnesses
the fervor of the people;
but since he has made us ready,
he has no idea where to go.

The easiest thing to carry is the one that is light
because it is empty.
That's why our President
has no trouble holding his head high.

Obama tried to prove to everyone
that he is not a camel.
We believed him . . . until he spit.

If Obama did not already exist,
he would have been created . . .
as a punishment for peoples' sins.

Obama has not yet achieved
a devilish power,
but he has already moved
far away from God.

Mr. Obama should be grateful
he is not crippled.
The Devil is missing one toe,
so Obama's fitness is proof
that, after all,
he can't be the Devil.

OBAMApower is the right to do evil,
supposedly for the betterment
of the society.

Obama is standing tall on the captain's deck
of a gigantic ship.
One can only hope that it is not a ship of fools.

The ship of state under Captain Obama
is heading for a shipwreck.

The higher the position, the wider the range of
vision and the more mistakes one can make.

When one declares a defeat as a success,
the situation must be deemed incurable.

Old saying:
It is easier to break something than to repair it.

To be big, powerful, a benefactor
of the humanity is the eternal craving of all the
small or those feeling small.
This is the Napoleonic syndrome.

Catching up to our President's promises is
impossible
even with the richness of the English language.

Our President has a Hollywood smile:
a lot of teeth and too little heart.

His word seemed to be cast in steel.
Unfortunately, it soon rusted.

Obama talks so much,
as if he swallowed a parrot.

Obama's tongue is so long,
it might be a good idea to tie it into a knot.

Maybe instead of trying to impress
the audience
with prerecorded jokes,
he will try to reach people with other means.

The two main illnesses
of politicians are:
unrestrained speech before elections,
and a loss of memory after.

Why does the President
have a tongue?
To hide his real thoughts.

Obama attracts people
with his lies because,
first of all, he believes in what he says.

The American President
has given
a thousand speeches
before coming out
from under the influence
of the dope of narcissism.

Sometimes mini brains
produce maxi lies.

How difficult it must be for Obama to stay silent
even when he has nothing to say.

Mr. Obama, you can lie only in moderation,
just as with using makeup . . . otherwise,
you lose the appearance of your face.

Obama always remains himself.
What an actor!

Facts are a stubborn thing . . .
but Obama is even more stubborn.

Why is it
that our President had his belly button
tied at birth, but not his tongue?

Our President promises everything
to everybody.
But there is a lot of "everybody"
and not enough of "everything."

Obama's pre-election speeches represent
the menu of anticipation.
Beware: these are only appetizers.
The main course will come later.

Reputation is not like the Pyramids of Egypt.
You can't build them on the shifting sands of
empty promises.

The worst of inflations are:
inflation of promises and
inflation of trust.

New expression: Lying as a teleprompter.
I have nothing against technology and progress.
I am simply against the progress of indecency.

Using a teleprompter is the easiest way to
proclaim oneself a genius.

Oh, how many soap bubbles
our President blew through
the fanfares of his microphone!

Soon, Obama's public speeches
will have such a smell,
that there will be a shortage of gas masks.

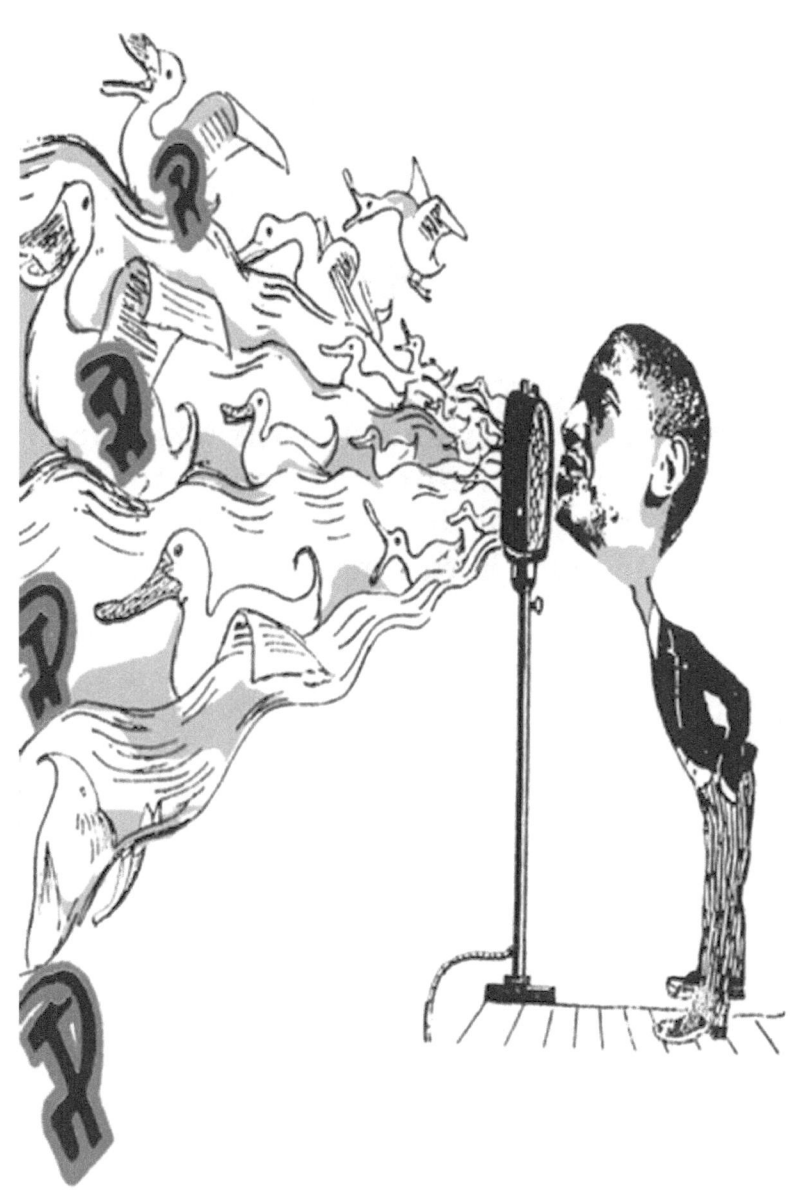

Our President is not only a master debater,
but also a political masturbator.

By the way,
the father of Socialism
did not have speechwriters and certainly
didn't know what a teleprompter is.

Keep in mind,
nothing is as cheap and yet costs us so much
as empty promises that tomorrow
life will be better than today,
and much better than yesterday.

With Obama's unity of thoughts, people
can exist even without thoughts.

Lies and conscience coexist well
as long as they sleep separately.

The impossible is possible.
The unthinkable is achievable.
What?—You don't believe it?
It's the essence of all the President's speeches.

Try to understand the essence
of Obama's speeches.
Remember that 80% of a human being is water.

Obama thinks
that the strength of his rules
is in the weakness of their perception

Grandeur does not have to be loud.
The greatest ocean is also the Pacific Ocean.

Mr. Obama is not a man of all talk.
The President can also add action
to some of his words.
This makes us very afraid.

Making sense of Obama's speeches
is equivalent to looking for colored pictures
in a volume written by Karl Marx.

When a wolf reads a sermon,
watch the sheep.

Definition of egocentric:
a person who reads nothing
but his own speeches.

A lie has short legs but such a long tongue.

The eagle is recognizable when it flies,
and the politician—when he lies.

Our Orator-in-Chief (Commander-in-Speech)
is very handy at talking.
But words do not spread readily on bread,
and people will get tired
of the same breakfast, lunch and dinner.

The President is trying
to feed society with promises,
but society is dying from hunger.

Listening to our President,
we begin to understand
that our future will be worse than the present.

Even nightingales fall silent
when our President sings.
That is because it is impossible
to sing and vomit at the same time.

According to the Bible, first came the word.
After the coming of Obama . . .
words, words, words.

The President lies and lies and lies . . .
But his lies are so straightforward.

Our President tried to teach the whole country
to speak with his Chicago accent.

Today our Performer-in-Chief is doing
what he does best: talking and mocking.

Beware of a person who constantly talks about
his noble ideas. He might steal from you.

Idol worship is a reminder of slavery;
soon, the number of worshipers
will become negative.

We must study the difference
between victory
and funeral marches.

Tubas are all the same,
but their music reflects
a different reality.
Therefore,
we are successfully moving ahead
on the economical and political cemetary.

The President thought
he was raising the victory flag,
but in reality,
it was a tag
for a gigantic short sale
of American values.

People die
under the flags of truth.
It is disgusting to live
under the flags of lies.

Let us be charitable to the rooster
that sings in the morning
thinking that he is causing the sunrise.

A rooster once tried to make the sunrise
come sooner by crowing longer and louder,
but he failed.
Knowing his imminent fate to end up
in a stewpot, he continued to sing . . .
his swan song.

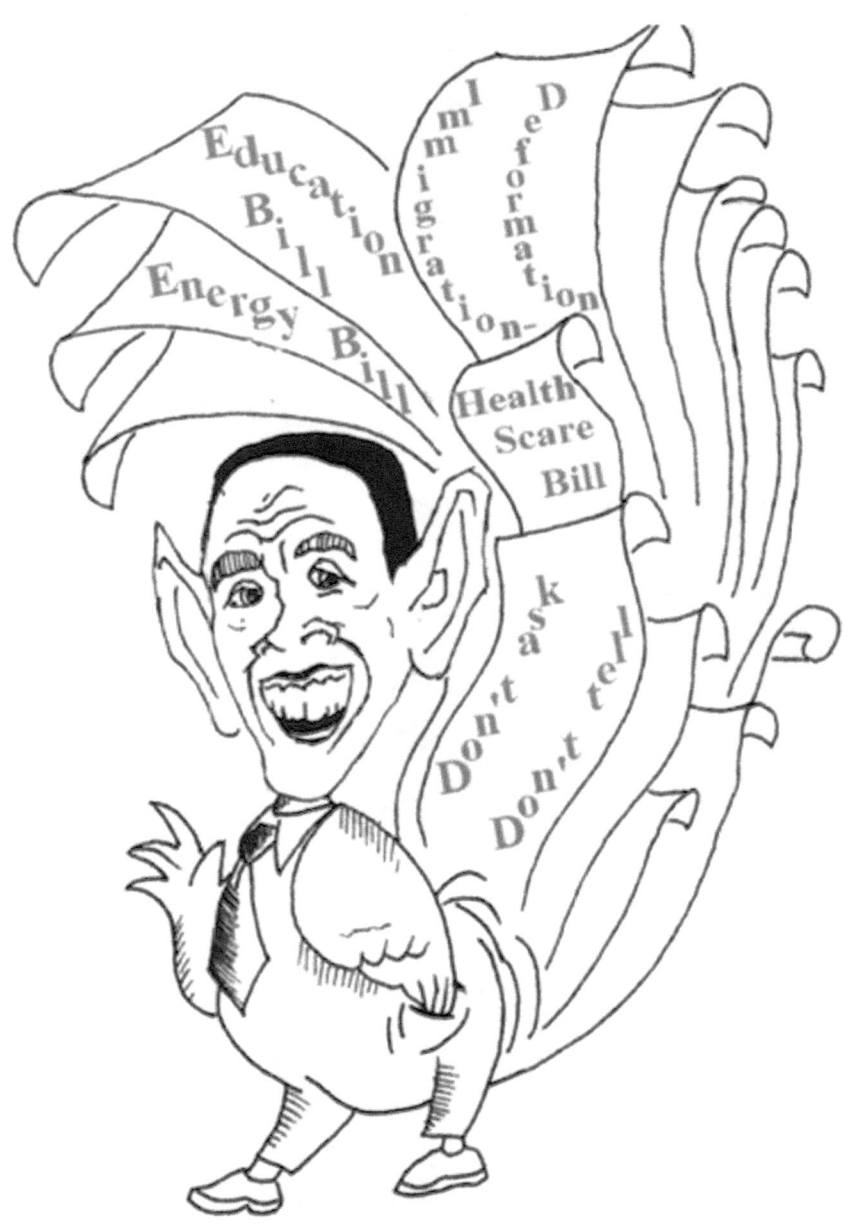

Mr. Obama very "respectfully" bowed
to the king of Saudi Arabia.
What can we do?
It's a habit, developed over the years.

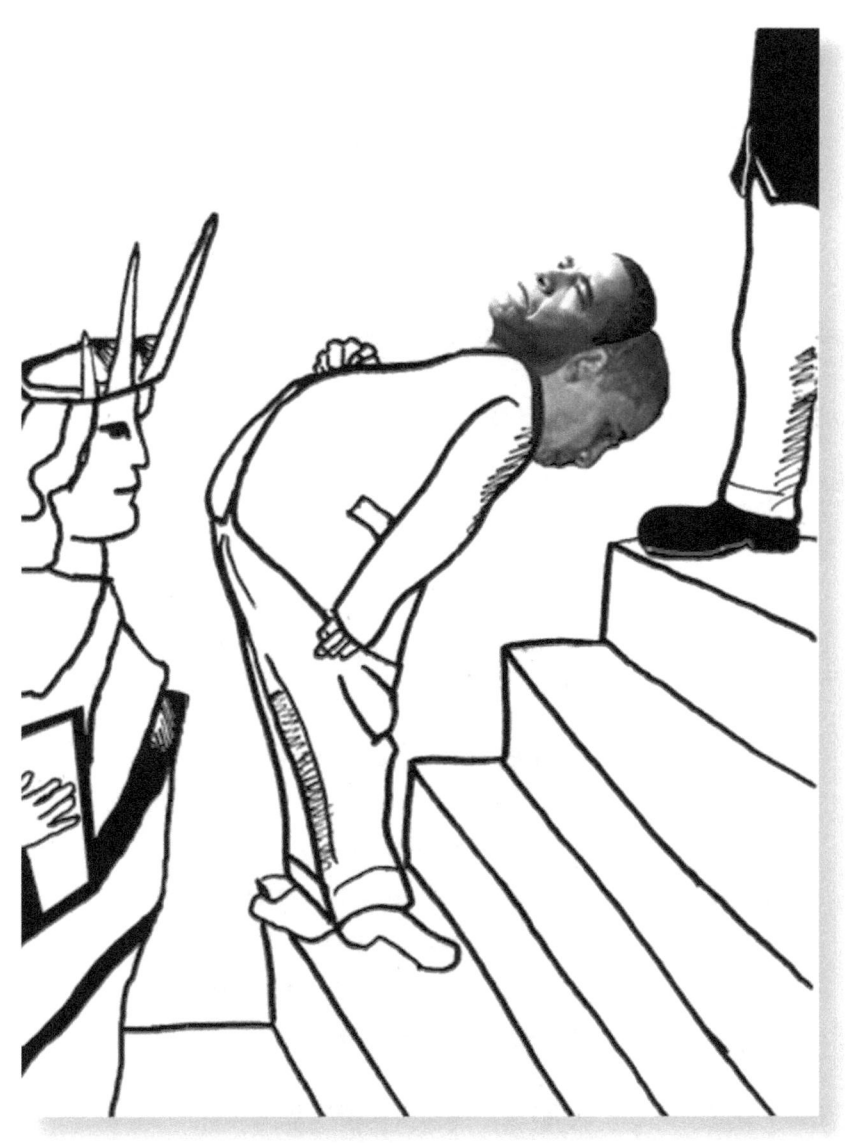

If you want to lick feet, do it,
but don't humiliate your home country
and your place under the sun.

Not so much likeable, as lickable.

Once, Obama bowed
to the Japanese Emperor
and hit his nose really hard.
"It must have been the floor," guessed Obama.
"It must be
an American public servant,"
guessed the Emperor.

Mr. President,
can you lick your back?

Sometimes an Achilles heel is located
inside a head.

Today people laud
Barak Hussein Obama
as the most decorated
crowd-pleaser in the world,
who entered history
from the back door.

Foreign dignitaries can celebrate
our chief of mischief
for his most notable achievement . . .
he is our first muslim-infected
first black, first red,
anti-American President.

The current resident
of the White House
will soon announce that
he is tired of being the President.
The coronation ceremony
is scheduled for April 1st.

Chapter 2
DEMONcRATS

People will be rewarded
for what they say,
and they will also be rewarded
for what they do.
                    Proverbs 12:14

Satire is a mirror
where the smart one sees himself
and a Democrat sees others.

When a large chunk of the country
screams "Hooray!"
I try to find the strength to whisper, "Help!"

A satirist tries
to awaken common sense among public
and conscience among politicians.

An avalanche starts from
the falling of one stone
but culminates in a major disaster.

America, be careful.
If you lose the face of freedom,
you will find yourself in a muzzle.

Americans are famous for their ability
to find a way out of most difficult situations,
but they are more famous for the ability
to find a way in there.

An aphorism is like a whistle
on a steam boiler that starts screaming
when everything inside is boiling,
although sometimes it screams beforehand.

The last one to laugh is the one
who is the first to shoot.
Let's protect the Second Amendment
of the Constitution
so we retain the right to shoot satiric barbs.

Satire's verdict is not subject to appeals.

Humor makes fun of inadequacies,
while satire cries at them.

Sometimes it takes the sourest-tasting pills
to provide the best results
in curing a sickness.

The diamond is forgiven for its sharp edges
because of its strength and beauty.

In a civil war, satire's role
is to be a barricade for the right cause.

Satire is a scalpel, belonging to a surgeon,
who is bravely fighting
the cancer of our society.

Satire is fine work performed with a scalpel
against a politician working with an axe.

Writing humor is an easy task for me . . .
just looking at our government helps
me enormously.

Laughter is a defense weapon
that protects society
so that a new idol does not appear
to take the place of the overthrown one.

When there is no satire permitted,
concentration camps appear.

Blown-up authorities are most afraid
of the sharp pen of a writer.

Obama found suitable people
and became their leader.
Socialists of various kinds surround
the President, kick him in the back
and give a motion to his trajectory.

If monkeys are our distant predecessors,
we are their shortsighted successors.

The higher the rank that a fool has, the
more meaningful is the foolishness
that he gets a chance to perpetrate.

I need to make appointments
with the eye and ear doctors.
I find a big difference between what I see
and what I hear.

From the levers of power, one
needs to take fingerprints.

In the crowd of lawmakers,
the plain honest face catches the eye. That
would be the face of a security guard.

Our Democrats are not as much lawmakers
as they are lawbreakers.

In the new laws,
passed by the Democratic Congress,
there can be too much sense,
but not a common one.

In our country new demo-laws are read
only by law-makers,
and they will be abided only by the brainless.

Democrats are sure
that they will be able to fulfill
and *over-fulfill* their ideals.

Democrats try to implement principles
of their ideology inside of people,
while always wearing them
outside as ties.

Democrats get real pleasure from their laws,
and the rest of the country
has nothing to do, but to accept the immoral.

The largest number of mirages exists
in the desert of the mind.

Nothing is as far from honor
as a Democratic code of honor.

The fools in our fairy tales are often smarter
than the fairy tales told by our fools.

A limited brain can still include
an unlimited quantity of bull . . .

During pressure-free elections,
Democrats elected slavery.

After the presidential election
I've got the impression, that
there are many
more Democrats than people in the world.
Is it not time to change the proportion?

The political arena is mined
with super promises,
on which our hopes will explode.

Our life is similar to the fall weather
in New York:
you believe one thing, hope for another,
and get yet a different one.

Democrats build castles in the air,
and the country is forced to live in them.

Our homegrown lefties view
the red flag of socialism
through the rose-colored lenses of idealism.

Democrats are unclear on the difference
between "Constitution" and "Prostitution."

Hope is the last thing to die.
The conscience is the first.

Obama puts his hopes on the shoulders
of those surrounding him.

The definition of Democratic Politics:
lies, justified by the people's interest.

There were suspicions about a politician,
that he was smart, experienced and honest.
But during the examination, no proof emerged,
so the suspicion of honesty no longer exists.

Democrats think that they are hackers
who hacked the personal website of God and
established an unlimited credit for themselves.

Chameleons are chosen to rule by those
who are color-blind.

The pluses of Democratic laws
are well-disguised minuses.

The politics of Democrats and conscience
are two lines that never intersect,
not even in infinity.

Dear Democratic Sirs:
Please save up the sands of your eloquence.
There is much more to be built on them.

When a Democrat announced
he was leaving politics,
the ovation was greater than any heard before,
even at the peak of his career.

Our task is to look the truth in the face . . .
preferably with a lot of humor.

We live in such times that the
avant-garde of our society brings up the rear.

If what Democrats are doing
is a scientific experiment,
why don't they first test it on rats?

The higher a Democrat climbs,
the more he wants to spit at those below.

Democrats can answer any question,
except the simple ones, like "Yes or No".

Democrats think the same way,
write with the same handwriting,
and speak in the same voice.

Sometimes Democrats swim differently,
but will sink the same way.

Not having a single original thought
yet managing to express oneself colorfully
is the reason why Democrats are successful.

Intelligence is required
for understanding one's own foolishness.
Democrats are not blessed with
such intelligence.

Democrats are characterized by a tendency
of replacing mistakes with other mistakes.
What kind of theater is it
where the actors applaud themselves?

Democrats' ideas should be walked out
on a leash and with a muzzle.

When fools achieve power,
they become scoundrels.

The caliber of a Democrat is
determined by how many people
he fools and for how long.

A Democrat is the one who drives those crazy
who are already that way.

If a defeat is declared a success,
this means it was a great defeat.

Is it reformation or deformation?

Not everyone who laughs
every minute is an optimist.
Some are Democrats.

Our country renders punishment
for individual crimes
and encourages collective crimes.

A band of reformists wants
to capture hostages:
350 million Americans.

The highest concentration
of reformers is found
in the psychiatric clinic.

Any human being can become a lawmaker,
But can a lawmaker become a human being?

It is not enough
to be descended from a monkey.
You also need to become a human.

Meeting a democratic congressman is similar
to reading a poisonous information booklet.

Our political situation is so funny
that we want to cry.

The skillfulness of Democrats
lies in their ability to exchange their
harpoons for Cupid's arrows,
a hit on the pocket for proof of love of society.

The silence of the lambs is evidence
that they are ready to become rams.

During the flood, blue dog Democrats
are the first to ring the warning bell . . .
but later fall asleep.

The Congress is playing their brand of baseball.
They have plenty of bats but no balls.

Statistically, 90 percent of those
who serve the people successfully, imitate
intellectual and physical labor.

Please do not worry
about a shortage of wood from the forests.
There is plenty of wood in the heads
of our legislators.

Scientists have proven
that the chemical makeup of Democrats
consists of 50 percent water and
50 percent lies.

For Democrats, a lie is simply self-defense.

The politics of Democrats differ
from pornography in that both are indecent,
but pornography at least
makes you want to participate.

Congratulations to those lawmakers
whose income exceeds one million dollars.
You automatically are enrolled
in the Affordable Housing Program.

When I watch a Congressional hearing
and listen to some of the decisions they make,
I am strongly in favor of hooking up
an electric current to some of those chairs.

We choose with our eyes closed,
not because we know much
about our candidates, but because we simply
prefer not to look at them too closely.

The Democrats' absence of principles
is the foundation of their physical wellness . . .
and their crippled conscience.

Free radicals endanger our life.
By the way,
let us call them "ridicules".
Why consider them Liberals
if they don't give a damn about
the liberty of the individual?
Why should we accept them
as Democrats, if they are deaf
to the voice of majority?
It may be proper
to recognize them as leftists,
ideologically crippled
left-brainers.

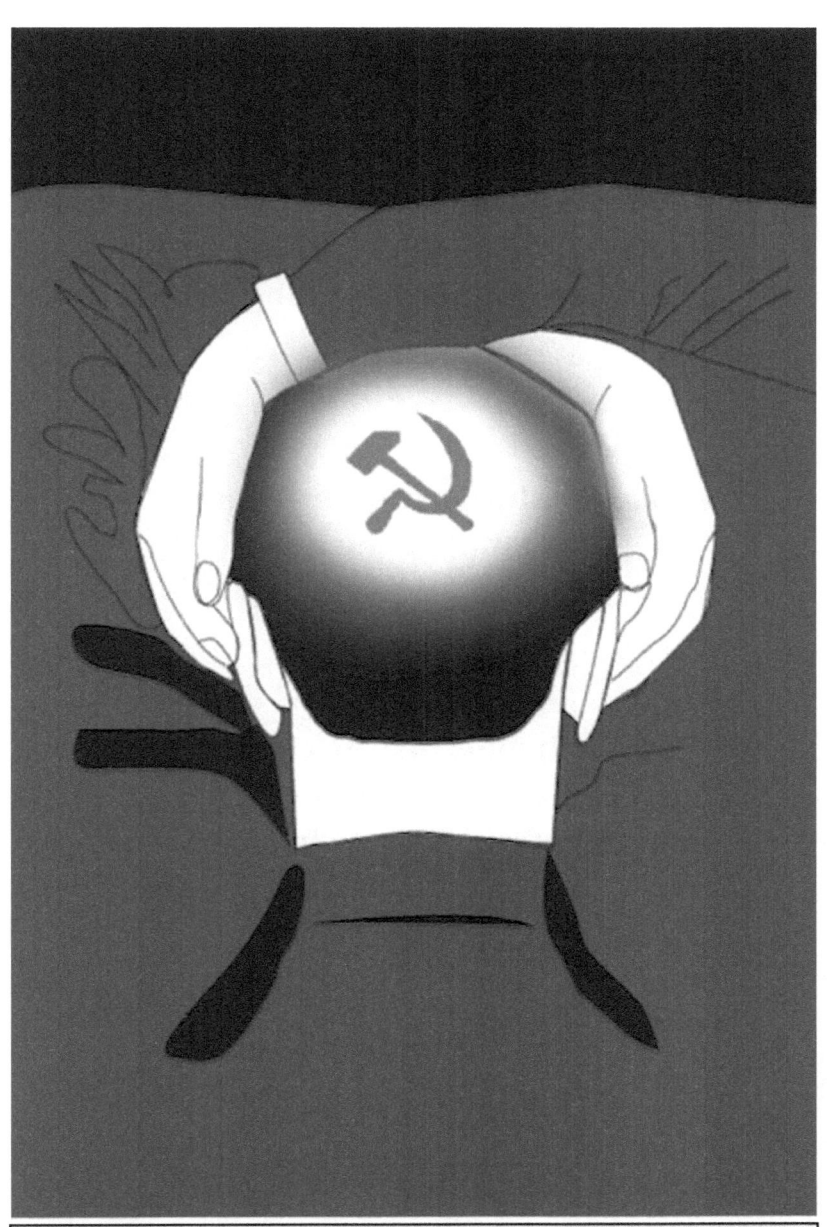

**Egotism and nihilism
Democrats view as patriotism.**

I disagree with the philosopher who said
that a mind is like a parachute;
if you don't use it, you'll fall and will be crushed
because some heads are filled with air
and can bounce for a long time.

The healthier the vocal cords,
the smaller the head.

Nothing brings people closer than
a common wrong that wins,
because of superiority in numbers.

A lie has a thousand of faces;
the truth has only one.

Some rely on the cult of power.
Others rely on power cults.

Today, people wait for what's been promised.
Then they will be preparing
for the next election.
Is it not time to stop waiting?

There is an old saying: "You reap what you sow."
America is a bountiful country,
we sowed Democrats into power and,
as a result,
we are harvesting taxes.

When Democrats touch the clean spots
of our civility,
they dirty them.

It is very likely that soon
the history of our country will be called
the "History of Illness."

Obama has managed
to achieve a downfall
without climbing a single summit.

Every new bill
is worse than an oil spill
and will of spending
will lead to economy bending.

The investigation
concerning disappearance
of money from Stimulus
provided sensational results:
it turned out that money was
periodically stolen
by Somali pirates.

Democrats have baked the most unsavory pie
and are forcing the people to eat it.

When cheese becomes more expensive,
mousetraps fill up with promises.

The war cry of Democratic cannibals is,
"You're either with us or . . . in the pot."

How beautifully the colors change
at the carnival of Democratic chameleons!

The election of a Democrat into Congress
is a fall upward.

Those who don't have a present
live in the future; those
who do not have a future live with the past.

The future is already not so great, because
Democrats started messing it up.

What we have now, ten years ago
was called "a bright future."
Ten years from now this will be called
our "beautiful capitalistic past."

The new, bright future of America
is even happier than the old,
bright future of Soviet Russia.

Our dark present
is the bright future of our fathers.
Do you understand where I am going with this?

Garbage never floats against the current.

In our society,
quantity is viciously attacking quality.
The results can be foreseen.

The idealism of Democrats
is American national foolishness.

To be "right" has two meanings.
One of them is "correct."
To be "left" also has two meanings.
One of them often precedes the word "behind."

No matter how alluring the desire
to be honest is; our legislators do
not succumb to it.

Incorruptible politicians do not exist.
There are only those who, as of yet, aren't
corrupted. Exceptions only confirm the rule.

What is the difference between the
notions "redistribution" and "theft"?
No difference.

Well-balanced politics comes about
when good intentions
are balanced out by bad decisions.

Our country elected Obama as President,
not because he was the candidate
who most voters looked up to,
but the one who the fewest looked down on.

Naive people trust the liars.
How could it be otherwise?
If it were not this way, liars
would be unable to lie.

The colder the political calculations are,
the hotter the outpouring.

When zeros are preceded by a one,
they should be considered respectfully.

Chapter 3
The goVERMINt

We respect the government
the same way it respects us.

In our country, there are no fools,
but there is a government.

Citizens, don't lie to yourselves! Let
government professionals do it.

The Obamists will try hard to force
into the heads of the public
the completely absurd thought that
"Motherland" and "Government" are
synonymous.
"Motherland" is a mother who gave us birth,
and "the Government" is a vehicle,
that hardly ever moves
in the same direction as the public interest.

Those who had ascended so high that
they achieved orbit are still subject to
the gravitational pull of satire.

The long-eared want to lead the short-minded.

When black is presented as white,
sometimes it all appears as grey . . .
and worse, sometimes, it all turns to red.

Our government has managed to find
a comfortable spot between the past
and the future.

The government threw us in the dump
and now is busy trying to convince us
that it smells good.

It is a disaster when people with the psychology
of a Mafioso are at the helm of the government.
In that case,
robbery is elevated to the rank of state policy.

The slogan of Obama's administration is:
"It may flood after us."
Though, in reality,
there will be a desert with no oases.

Which is more important:
That competent, honorable people
govern the country,
or that we believe it is so?

The definition of catastrophe
is when people with the philosophy of robbers
get access to power.

The branches of the government
are twisted and dragged down
by the weight of their rotting fruit.

The branches of the government should not
shield people from the sun of freedom.

The Democratic baseball bat
aspires to play the role
of a conductor's baton.

Government and people
are different civilizations.

The only thing our government
is ready to sacrifice in it's fight
for the people, *is* the people.

Some have a humane attitude
toward animals;
others have an animalistic attitude
toward humans.

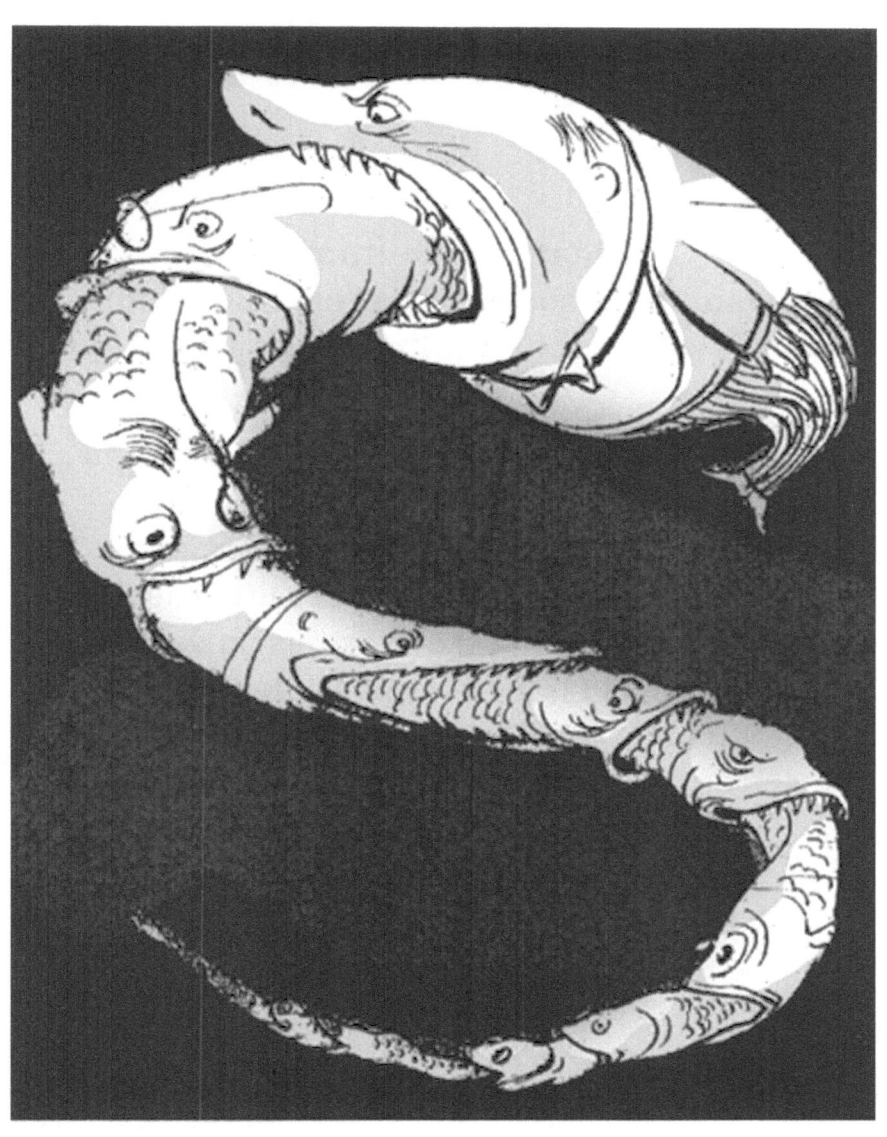

Government at work.

If it were not for the society,
the government would have no problems.

Today, the government
is standing in society's way of seeing things.
Soon, it will start forbidding the society to look.

Millions of bureaucratic representatives
put all their strength to get to the trough,
while pushing the previous power
as far away as possible.
They decided to get to the trough
at any price . . .
even at the cost of their grandparents
and children.

It is clear today that keeping good relationships
with social fascists and terrorists is the same as
flirting with an alligator.
And why does it open its mouth?
To smile or to eat you alive? Tickling
it to make it feel good is useless. It's much
easier to hit it on the head.

Congress is a herd in which
every sheep considers itself
a shepherd.

We, all of us, are the foundation of the bridge
that the Government crosses
on its way to prosperity . . . its own.

It is untrue that in our Government
there are only indecent people.
Let's be objective—
some of them are incompetent as well.

The most beautiful tunes come from people
who do not attempt to conduct them.

Obama's government will drown in lies . . .
and soon.

In a country under foolish management,
April Fool's Day comes not just once a year
but every day.

In our country, corruption is growing
with its roots upward.

Our government consists of true gentlemen
with old traditions.
They do not know how to earn money,
but they do know how to spend it.

Our government is controlled by the people
who are like passengers that not only decide
where to go, how to get there,
and how to operate the means
of transportation,
but also grab the controls, confusing the brakes
and the accelerator in the process.

The purpose of governmental socialistic
experiments is to see whether
it is possible to make our situation even worse.

When talking about the government
tell the truth or remain silent.
It is just like speaking about the dead.

Our country is in its deepest crisis,
for our people there is nothing left to lose
except our Government.

Just say "No"!

What is the meaning of socialized medicine?
The same as a subsidized funeral . . .
Or a placebo, presented as a wonder drug.

Health care is a large part of our economy
so nothing revives economic
desert as a colorful mirage.

Soon America will turn into
a mental institution where from the first
impression everyone is well, a crazy house,
where patients make their own prescriptions.

Socialist universal health care idea
is a theory of probability applied to society.
As a result, soon our national anthem
will soon sound like a song:
"So long liberty, so long bravery, hello slavery . . ."
and the address of the world-famous collective
farm will be the slaughter house
of the Soviet Union of America.

Soon in our sick society,
the healthy ones will be put in isolation.

A sick socialist's alienated brains cannot
create an effective health care system.
As a result, health care reminds
one of *hell* care, or health *scare.*

Unattainable Presidential plans
are nevertheless grandiose.

An apple fell on Newton's head, and
he discovered the law of gravity.
What fell on Obama's head
when he "discovered"
the concept of universal health care?

A mouse is giving birth to a mountain.
Shall we laugh?

Who wants to read
a newly released fiction novel
"How to Reform the Entire Health System?"

What is the difference between disaster and
catastrophe? Introduction of the universal
health care bill was a disaster.
The implementation of the bill
will create a catastrophe.

The law concerning socialized medicine
is one of the cruelest laws concerning
a good thing.

Political xylophone,
Democratic obamaphone.

If, under the current health care system,
there is a shortage of funds,
under the new system there
will be a shortage of care.

The Surgeon General of Common Sense warns,
"Soon the government health care system
will be dangerous to the health of the people,
and life in America will be dangerous to our
lives."

The President has decided
to make our citizens happy
with enhanced government care on April 1st.
The grateful people decided to thank
the government
by paying taxes also on April 1st.

In the so-called "beautiful building"
of universal socialized medicine,
the biggest room will be the waiting room.

Our new health care system will
make us blissful with open-to-the-public
open heart surgeries,
tooth extractions without anesthesia,
euthanasia of those who don't want it,
and a complimentary DVD of Obama's speeches
for each patient.

7

Government to retirees:
"Let's make a deal: we will extinguish you,
and you in turn will praise and love us."

State-subsidized health care resembles
swimming in a pool without the water.
It's difficult at first, but eventually
you get used to it.

State border lines of our country are easily
violated by illegals, while the stupidity
of the state healthcare plan has no borders.

If all donkeys decide to start
living as people do,
then all people will start living like donkeys.

Socialized medicine remains
an enhanced technique of discrimination
against the elderly.
It is close to the final solution
of aging problems.

Socialized medicine is not the homicide
of the younger generation.
It's simply the ultimate form of rudeness.

In the trend of social care living, we
will get neither care or the living.

There is not only cheese in the medical
mousetrap, but also holes that come with it.

Is it possible for a dog to suffer a heart attack?
Sure, if you make the dog live like people do.

The time of our golden age is a brilliant dusk.

Our society, as our new health care system,
resembles the blooming yet rotting tree.

Obama's medical reform will teach patients
to get sick only on specified days,
and by appointment only.

Our youth has fewer and fewer chances
to die before they are old.

If the case must be amended,
it means that it is ailing.

The desire to stand until death
is blocked out by the desire to survive.

With regard to the new health care system,
it's best to remain healthy.

Fresh, healthy, and gone crazy.

Many hope
that with regard to the new health care system,
it could regretfully be said,
"Finita la Commedia."
I don't really believe in this.
I am sure that we'll be forced to say,
"Perpetuum Mobile."

Shut your mouth
and scream as hard as you can!

The most horrible result
of socialized medicine
is the creation of a culture of
beggars and order-takers.

Giving up free choice and related responsibility
will destroy the foundation of America
and make our Founding Fathers
turn over in their graves.

Soon in our country, anything will be allowable,
except three things:
to be born, to live, and to die.

The incurable illnesses
have a great future.

Health scare bill

General belief in illusions
is a beginning of delusions.

116

Don't think what your government
xcan do for you.
Think what you can DO
for your government.

Chapter 5
FREAKonomics

"You shall not covet." (10)
"You shall not steal." (8)
Exodus 20: 1-17

I hope our government
will be capable
of counting up to
the Ten Commandments.
Satirist General

This morning I woke up with a smile
on my face. I had a dream:
President Obama came up to me and asked,
"How much money do I owe you?"

There are no situations
that do not have a solution.
One can always declare bankruptcy.

You can take in a great deal of water
and still suffer from thirst.

Nothing clears vision better
and unites people more than when they see
that someone is going after their pockets.

Nothing separates people more than ideology,
and nothing unites them
more than appetite.

**Optimism of Obamism
ultimately becomes social idiocy.**

We are not only the children of our time;
we are also its parents.

Redistribution of wealth is an attempt
to force everyone to eat at the same trough.

Because of new reforms and taxes,
our society of consumers
will become a nudist society.

It is now an open hunting season on
millionaires and billionaires.
Who is the next prey?

We need to listen to the voice of reason.
Of all voices speaking to us, it is the quietest.

While laughing, people let go of their past,
so they can cry about the present
and be horrified by their future.

At the bottom of our promised heaven,
we can find unexpected hell.

In science, paradox plays a big role.
The same is true about politics,
economics, and morals.

The road to paradise is paved with good
intentions . . . that have been steamrolled over
by the so-called "do-gooders."

Obama decided to make
the rate of unemployment half of what it is
by showing up on TV twice as often.

What is the difference between USA and Kenya?
There isn't any,
except that Kenya has no nuclear weapons.

To open the eyes of idealistic Americans,
I suggest a couple of trips to Cuba.

Wealth isn't determined
by how much you spend,
but by how much you save.

Runaway socialism
can capitalism.

Why is there such a long line of people
waiting to see the eye doctor?
According to the President, everyone must see
that our economy is beginning to grow!

The whole country is suffering from vision
problems: we just cannot see any money!

Our soap opera is flourishing.
One part of the economy that's certainly risen
is the growing production of soap bubbles.

The Democrats tell people:
"There are two ways to bring the country
out of its current economic crisis.
Either Martians will land on Earth and assist us,
or we will do it on our own.
The second option is absolutely unfeasible!"

Looking at our situation, we have to admit
that the sausage is hanging higher and higher,
while our citizens,
thanks to additional taxation,
have become shorter and shorter.

We need to wake the people up and rally
against Obama's economic reform. One
possible method
is to televise a portion
of Charlie Chaplin's "Gold Fever"
the part where hungry Charlie eats a boot.

Recently, my neighbor approached me
with a question:
"I heard on TV that the President proclaimed
the recession is almost over,
and that productivity is growing.
Yet I am still unemployed and
my refrigerator is empty!"
My response:
"Connect your TV to the refrigerator,
but don't rely on pie in the sky."

"Citizens, tighten up your belts
and prepare for a bumpy ride"
—is the concise meaning
of most anti-crisis plans of our government.

The government proposes
that the unemployed take courses
of a different specialty
but the only course that people want to take
is the one about raising wages.

The unemployed are pleased not only by
the decrease of queue in front of them,
but also by a significant increase
of the line behind them.

According to the Government,
the recession is over.
Only a few details remain.
Those "details"
will be more damaging
than the whole recession.

No matter what you do to a person,
he stubbornly persists in believing
in a better future.

There is only one thing worse
than an empty stomach—an empty brain.

Global warming is a result of human attempts
to worsen the life on Earth.

The establishment of a new presidential entity
in our country is usually
the result of printing too much money.

In our country, the general aroma is the smell of money,
and our tax money turned into pork.

There are two major problems
in our country: fools and crooks.
Unfortunately, each one of these problems
is trying to find a solution
at the expense of the other.

Soon smart businessmen
forecasting the rise and fall of the dollar ...
will demand payment in yuans.

The recession will end soon.
It's impossible for the situation
to remain so sad
and so laughable at the same time.

The shortest American joke:
all of the so-called "too big to fail"
repaid their debts to the people.

American democratic paradox:
we have thirty six czars, and
all of them are Democrats.

We in the United States surpass the world
in our number of czars.
It would not hurt to fall behind
in the number of idiots.

Even the Pope,
God's representative on Earth, is chosen,
yet our czars are appointed.

Shadows always march side by side,
so thirty six czars comprise a platoon.

A whole choir of czars
cannot mute the murmur of the truth.

Our economy has thirty
six nannies—czars
-and is still unattended.

The appointment of the auto industry czar
was based on the discovery
of old General Motors parts in his blood vessels.

Our green czar
has turned out
to be quite red.
Too bad our President is color-blind.

When you reach into someone else's pocket,
it is a **theft**.
When you break into someone's home,
it is a **robbery**.
When part of the society
is robbed based on
social and economic principles,
it is **redistribution**.
And when people
are robbed for "their benefit",
it is **taxation**.
If some citizens produce treasure bills,
it is a **crime**.
If the government overprint trillions
of phony dollars,
it is **inflation**.

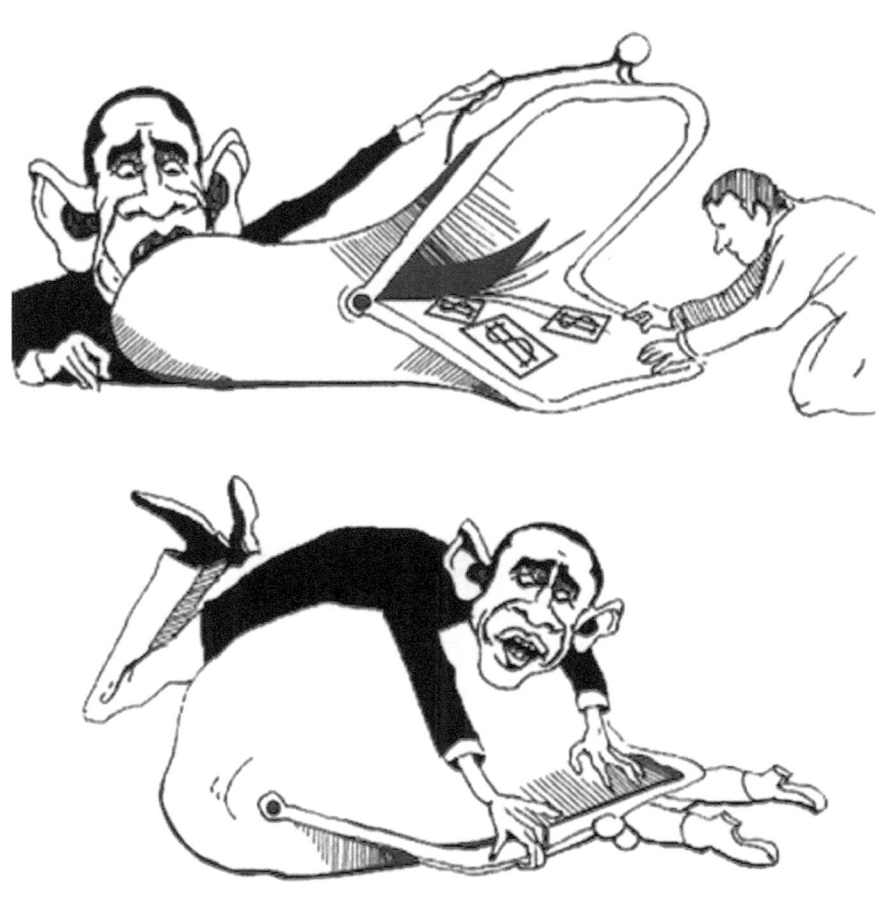

In order to be a true saint,
one has to either be Jesus
or pay all the taxes.

If the country continues having
setbacks in employment,
it's possible the country will be impregnated
with revolution.

Double-digit inflation is imminent.
Prices will grow without restraint.
The only things that will remain unchanged
during the current President
are mileage, hours, and pounds of promises.

Next year, government promises
to stabilize the dollar.
And if possible, even two.

Our fathers spilled their blood for the future.
And what are we doing for our children?
We are spending their money non-stop.

Dreams that come true are plans.
Dreams that don't come true are
either illusions or delusions.

Inflation

Let us be economical
with the tool of optimism
so that it lasts until the end of the year,
when pessimism
will overcome us once again.

To spend our money reasonably,
the government needs only two things.
Guess which ones.

Whose fault is it that we are unable
to produce and export anything,
except paper bills?

Economists answer questions
not because they
know the answers,
but because they are asked.

The ship of our economy ran into the sandbar
and is now dreaming about the flood of money.

In politics, the winner usually
is not common sense;
it's common appetite.

Our President's program is quite peculiar.
To fight the nation's battle with obesity,
which the medical community has lost,
he used economy.
Therefore
dear countrymen, tighten your belts
and get used to it.

The true value of things becomes clear
when they disappear.
We will be sorry when free
enterprise disappears.

When war is declared on palaces,
huts burn down first.

The State is the Titanic
that started leaking from the top.

If the country is the Titanic,
and runaway spending is an iceberg, the Titanic is
guaranteed to sink.

Economic delusions begin
with political illusions.

The government is convincing us
that the more money we spend,
the faster we will solve
our economic problems.
Imagine if individuals started
using such recipes
in their own lives.

Spending Monster of our economy—
Stimulus, "sinmulus," "stealmulus,"
and the money printing
will invite the Monster of inflation.

Economic recovery went on for two years
And then depression started. "Stimulus
ran out," guessed Obama.

Fighting the recession
using economic stimulus and TARP
is like fighting plague with cholera.

A couple more rounds of stimulus
and there will be no money
left in the treasury to pay
for the Country's mere existence.

Economic stimulus
is our government's way
to fight the erectile dysfunction of our economy.
Unfortunately, it doesn't work that way.

Stimulus will help our economy
the way Viagra helps an Egyptian mummy.

Stimulus injections resemble swine infection.

While stimulus sounds very good on paper,
it is paper and not stimulus.

Transition to the new economic policy
begins from the period of romance,
which gradually evolves
into a period of dissonance.

If you want to be optimistic today,
do not look into tomorrow.

For bad people to be able to steal a lot,
good people have to work a lot.

Those who are naïve view the horizon
as their future.

Not everything is as bad as it seems.
Some things are far worse!

Never assume that things cannot get worse.
Wait until tomorrow,
and you will see that they have
become even worse than yesterday.

According to the President,
we have reached the bottom.
I feel that tomorrow the bottom
will be even deeper.

Today, we experience
an apocalyptic unemployment situation,
hunger, moral downturn, wars, etc.
Is it not the perfect time
for the Messiah to come?
The only problem is finding a suitable jackass,
because all of them are busy in the Congress.

The Obamists boast
that they rescued our society
from the economic noose.
Please don't push us into the abyss.

The socialistic desert views a capitalistic oasis
as a dirty spot on its reputation.

A country in the state of depression
considers suicide as an ultimately
optimistic idea.

Today in America. creditors have to live long.

Our country is a motherland of
entrepreneurship. Now it's becoming
entrepreneurship's "graveland".

If the recession turned into depression
and then into diarrhea,
don't despair, it will only complicate
the situation.

"We will make your celebration unforgettable:
birthdays, weddings, corporate parties . . ."
Sincerely, the IRS

This year, President Obama decided
to decorate the Washington Christmas tree
with figurines of the unemployed.

Do you have problems with debt?
Have you lost your job? We will help you.
The Democratic Parachute Club

How come that when the people earn money,
the government takes it away?
That's because the government earns money by
taking away what others have earned.

It seems as if our budget was created
by the plant that manufactures
gigantic rubber balloons.

Uncovering individual shortcomings
of our economy is as pointless
as trying to fix one hair instead
of the entire bad hairdo.

A good recipe against economic problems—
to sit in warm pants on a cold stove—
doesn't help but doesn't hurt and costs nothing.

Based on the public opinion,
the rich cause all our troubles.
But if they are so bad,
why do all the poor people try to become rich?

Congress gave birth
to a Godzilla-like deficit.
Who is the father?

The Egyptian pyramids
were built on slaves' bones.
Our current economy,
on the bodies of naïve idiots.

We got what we asked for,
but certainly not
what we expected.

CHANGE
HAS
COME

Atlases are becoming smaller.
Earlier on, they held the sky,
now, they are holding the balcony,
on which Obama speaks.

The idea of equality allows a lazy bastard
to climb on the back
of a hard worker and take away
the best of what he created.

Our recession and double-digit inflation
are the same
as *l'amour de trois* without the *amour*.

Democracy for Americans is a way of freedom.
But not just freedom, but freedom of money.
Not just any money, but only dollars.

Happiness is not only having money,
but also possesing it in quantity.

Mrs. Obama helps fight recession by planting
a garden in front of the White House.

The enemy of the state number two, the
Colorado Bug, is unsuccessfully trying to
stop abundance in our country.

The economy in America is similar to a war
that is impossible to win.

If your phone is disconnected, it means
the phone company played a joke on you.
If your lights are off, the electricians are joking.
If it happens with your water, electricity, phone
and gas at the same time,
it means the government finally recognized
your sovereignty.

Obama's economy is the economy that
was given green light, but instead it
went on red.

During hyperinflation,
a Democrat, in response to voters
demanding pay raises, says:
"My dear voters, why do you need so much
money? You already carry it
in baskets and groceries in your wallets."

The chimera that brings income
is global warming.

Our economy is healthy. However, the
straight line on the EKG causes
concern.

The biggest economic and political failures
are referred to as experiments
with new reforms.

Let's experiment, but not conduct any
experiments with red excrement.

The expected portrait of our economy:
wild moneys are swirling around
in an empty virtual space.

For their party meetings,
the insurance company executives have rented
a well-known retreat.
The next one will be in Buckingham Palace.

While observing the increase of prices,
you stop dreaming about immortality.

Inflation is when you need much more money
than before, just to see that happiness
is not in quantity, but in quality.

At the end of the tunnel,
instead of the expected light
there could be a dead end.

Today, the entire country lives for tomorrow.
Too bad that it is at the expense of today.
Although, tomorrow our children will suffer
as a result of what their parents did today.

Dear fellow middle class men,
sleep in peace with the accompaniment
of the government singing "Sleep, my Baby".
Your President will deliver prosperity
directly into your bed.

"Don't worry, be happy";
the nightmare will eat you only in reality.
The government is taking care of you
days and nights.

Fighting the recession
the "Obama way"
is like running in the same spot.

Inflation is coming and soon we,
people of Earth, will have to get used
to astronomic prices.

Forecasts can be of 3 types:
right, wrong, and Democratic.

Efforts to green up socialist deserts
usually end up
in devastation of capitalist oases.

Chapter 6
Our Home-Grown
SOSial Obamism

> *You sinners, clean sin
> out of your lives.*
> ### *James 4:7-8*

Aphorisms are my attempt
to hammer a wooden stake
into America's resurrected socialism.
Please read them in the daytime. It
is too scary to read them at night.

Obamism is incomparable
with sharp truth, reflected in satire.

Use these satiric shots
for protection
from the idiotism of Obamism.

Obama is armed with socialist ideas
and is very dangerous.

Obama's socialism
may not be the end of the world, but
why attend the dress rehearsal?

The ghost of socialism,
travelling across the world,
was looking for Marx but found Obama instead.

Socialism cares about a person,
as a train cares about somebody,
which it just ran over.

When a socialist charismatic leader
starts to rule a nation,
applause of victims turns into ovation.

Socialism is the system under which
people think that they
have received the government of the people,
by the people, for the people . . .
but in reality,
it is the people for the government.

Socialist darkness spreads
with the speed of light.

The only exit from a hopeless situation
is to get out through the same entrance
by which you came in.

Our naïve society rattles of socialism,
but it still hasn't been taken
from the nursing breast of capitalism.

Obamistic future will certainly be fair,
because by then there will be nothing
for us all to share.

Ideological dregs were poured
into the river of our society,
and the public took it for a new stream.

How terrible the parents of socialism are:
its mother is anarchy and its father is chaos.

The greatest accomplishment
of the socialist dinosaurs
is in the fact that almost all of them died out.
I hope history will repeat itself.

Obama's originality starts with
a long-forgotten discovery.

New reforms are old news,
even though they happen each time
with new people.

It is not enough
to create a crack
in the wall of capitalism
in the interest of planting the pretty-looking
garden of socialism.
Don't let the falling fragments crush you.

Those who will survive socialism
will tell stories
about how good things were under capitalism.

Capitalism starts with burglary
and ends with corruption.
Obamism starts
with both burglary and corruption;
what it will end with, only God knows.

We are not the first and not the last
to reclaim the path to socialism—
a path that leads nowhere.

The stain of our history starts
to gain a strong tint of red.

A socialist pyramid:
a son is sitting on the neck of his father,
who sits on the neck of the society.

Socialism is a type of religion
that promises celestial manna on Earth
and in the nearest future.

People must believe in a bright future;
otherwise,
they would demand a bright present.

People: while descending from heaven to Earth,
don't forget to open your parachutes.

To choose to be naked is nudism.
To lose one's clothes
is the result of Obama's socialism.

Is true socialist equality even possible?
When and where was there ever a fruitful desert?

Speaking of deserts brings to mind mirages.
Socialism is one of such mirages.
The closer you get to it, the farther away it is.

Nothing new happens
when you place a new monument
on an old pedestal.

If a drunkard loses his appreciation
of a fine wine,
he becomes an alcoholic.
If a human being loses his appreciation of
freedom, he becomes a slave.

The average person wants everything
and right away.
The typical person under socialism receives
nothing and gradually.

The true fool is one who strives
to achieve equality with smart ones.

Our President will successfully open
the heavenly gates of socialist hell.

Even if the President's road leads nowhere,
at least there is always green light on it.

As long as people can lie to themselves,
no truth will scare them.
If a comedy remains in production too long, it
becomes a tragedy.

With socialism resurrected,
not everyone has realized yet
that it is a mummy.

Socialism is similar to HIV:
there is a smaller number of those afflicted
than those infected.

I want to believe that the theory
of socialist absolutism of Marx
will not win over
the theory of capitalist relativity of Einstein.

It is laughable
that sometimes a socialist rattle believes itself
to be a refreshing thunderstorm.

Do not rush to either the cemetery or socialism
without first finding out the cost.

Only the Devil knows how to end up
in a socialist heaven.

The life we have now is by no means sweet,
but I'm sure that our descendents will envy us.

Chapter 7
God Save America . . .
From Ourselves.

> *You,*
> *my brothers [and sisters],*
> *were called to be free.*
>   *Galathians 5:13*

Satire is a mirror where a Democrat sees
a Republican and a Republican sees a Democrat

Democrats complain that Republicans
viciously attack them, builders of socialism, when
all they are trying to do is peacefully
and comprehensively engage
in destroying the capitalist system,
freedom, and American traditions.

Republicans and Democrats love to state:
"American people want this, American
people want that . . ."
Is it not time to stop guessing
and start working?

Democrats are trying to take the bull
by its horns,
while Republicans are going to
take the donkey by the ears.

If you ride a donkey, you will get
its stubbornness.
If you ride an elephant, you will get its strength.

For people it is the same—an elephant
in a china shop or a donkey in a candy shop.

A Republican would gladly extinguish a fire
in the White House with the help of my aphorisms.

I'm afraid that soon indifferent and blind
citizens will be guided not
by the rule of law but by special escort.

It's a grim possibility that after November,
Republican Winnie-the-Pooh will fall asleep
and Democrat Piglet as a decent pig,
will use the moment.

If my aunt had a beard she would be an uncle;
if a Democrat had balls
he would be a Republican.

There will be no civil war. Civilians are gone.
Those left here are merely inhabitants.

Question: "When will there be a better time?"
Answer of a Republican: "It already was."

The stub is proud of its roots;
Republicans are proud of their past.

A Democrat is a villain who thinks
that he became like that due to Republicans.

An optimistic Democrat: "One can always
squeeze a bit of shaving cream out of a practically
empty tube to shave all the wishful".
An optimistic Republican:
"There will be enough cream
'till we get another tube".

A Republican is a person who believes
that if one drops a slice of bread which is spread
with butter on both sides, it will hang in
the air not having decided on which side to fall.
A Democrat is sure that having fallen on the
floor, the bread will jump
and fall on the floor again
but on the other side.

During recession
a pessimistic Republican
is a well-informed optimist
and an optimistic Democrat
is a well-instructed and brainwashed pessimist.

The President addressed the Congress:
"Let's divide responsibilities
between Democrats and Republicans.
Republicans will convince
the rich to give money
and Democrats will convince
the poor to take it."
That will reflect bipartisan relations.

Democrats believe in a happy world ending,
Republicans believe in absolutely nothing.

For the well-being of our motherland
Democrats are ready
to lie down on the rails
or to put Republicans there.

In politics as in sex
your choice of a partner is all-important.

Wise Republicans will drink vodka
on the graves of the Democrats
who wanted to drink free champagne.

A Republican sees a tunnel.
A Democrat sees light at the end of the tunnel. An
independent sees a tunnel, light and a train.
A machinist sees these three idiots
sitting on the rails.

The American dream of the Republicans:
to win billions.
The Democrats' dream
is to spend billions.

I don't see a leader
in the Republican party;
the party reminds me
of a fly without a head,
that as if not noticing it,
proceeds to spin buoyantly and fly and buzz.

A Democrat: "Did you see
the President holding out
an olive branch of collaboration
to you, Republicans?"
A Republican: "Did you notice
the big fist holding that branch?"

To lower an elephant to the level of a donkey
makes him not only look ridiculous—
means to help him lose his ability to get things done.

All the candidates from all the parties promise
to struggle for and struggle against . . .
As a satirist advises,
one shouldn't struggle for cleanliness,
one should just wipe.

"Time heals," said a Democrat.
"Only if the illness is youth and not stupidity,"
replied a Republican.

Republicans sometimes also play dumb,
but it's very difficult
to compete with Democrats.

Division of duties in Congress: some crow,
while others promise to create a sunrise.

Democrats' tactics:
we know how, but don't know what.
Republicans' strategy:
we know what, but don't know how.

If a Democrat bites a Republican
this will not be shown on TV,
but if a Republican bites a Democrat
this has public interest.

How can Republicans gain a majority
in the Congress?
Pray that God will send
a meteorite to the left side of the aisle.

Democrats see straws in Republicans' eyes,
without noticing logs in their own.

According to Republicans our dark, capitalist
past will be America's bright future.

According to Democrats, Soviet red past
will soon be our bright future.

Democrats are our tactical weapon,
and Republicans—strategic.

2010

Sometimes, some Republicans
are quite silly;
sometimes, some Democrats
are notable for their intelligence.

Democrats dream to open the door
to a socialist future,
while Republicans dream to close the doors
after Democrats.
So the beginning of the deeds are in the hands
of Democrats, while the end—in Republicans'.

Republicans and Democrats are busy
defending democracy from each other.

A war is elimination of lawful
relationship between struggling parties.

I propose that American people
rise to the level of my aphorisms
and start acting.

When draught or fire came,
jungle inhabitants didn't attack each other—
danger brings animals together.

KATZStradamus:
Republicans and Democrats,
we are all covered in s . . . .

Republicans and Democrats,
duped and robbed citizens,
unite in struggle for our motherland!

Americans want to believe
that the battle between
Republicans and Democrats
will end in the victory
of the referee: the citizens
of the United States.

America's concerned citizens
don't want to see
"As Our Motherland Turns"
to Wonderland, Slanderland, Moronland,
Zombieland—
divided state
of Socialist Banana Republic.

2012

The paraphrase of the thought from
The Little Prince, by Antoine de Saint Exupéry:

If you love somebody, you are responsible
for them; if you love your garden and notice
weeds growing up and attempting to destroy
the beautiful flowers on your land, fight
the grass; save your flowers. Children,
thankfully, will enjoy the beautiful garden.

When our beautiful homeland is in the
midst of economic, political and military fires,
it is not the time for redecoration.
When so-called socialistic "high morality"
is turned into the high mortality, there won't be
time for consolidation and mobilization.
Time is running out. We live on a volcano,
and we must be prepared for a fight.
Talk peace, but keep your ammunition
ready. We are the most patient and generous
country in the world, but kindness
in our difficult time requires strong fists.
Gloves off, America—time to stand tall
in defense of our values, our civilization
and the future of our children.
"If not we, who else? If not now, then when?"

Praise the Lord. Respect the Constitution.
Look the truth directly in the eye.
"And truth will set you free".

Please send your inquiries and comments to:
www.obamasutrabook.com